MILLIONAI
THE SIMPLE HABITS AND T
WEALTH, A^

MILLIONAIRE MINDSET
THE SIMPLE HABITS AND THINKING BEHIND
MONEY, WEALTH, AND SUCCESS

CONTENTS

Chapter 1. WHO IS A MILLIONAIRE? 11
Chapter 2. WHAT IS A MILLIONAIRE MINDSET AND HOW IS IT ACQUIRED? 22
Chapter 3. WHY CHOOSE THE MILLIONAIRE MINDSET? 42
CONCLUSION 49

Copyright 2018 by Zen Mastery - All rights reserved

This document is geared towards providing exact and reliable information in regards to the topic and issue covered. The publication is sold with the idea that the publisher is not required to render accounting, officially permitted, or otherwise, qualified services. If advice is necessary, legal or professional, a practiced individual in the profession should be ordered.

- From a Declaration of Principles which was accepted and approved equally by a Committee of the American Bar Association and a Committee of Publishers and Associations.

In no way is it legal to reproduce, duplicate, or transmit any part of this document in either electronic means or in printed format. Recording of this publication is strictly prohibited and any storage of this document is not allowed unless with written permission from the publisher. All rights reserved.

The information provided herein is stated to be truthful and consistent, in that any liability, in terms of inattention or otherwise, by any usage or abuse of any policies, processes, or directions contained within is the solitary and utter responsibility of the recipient reader. Under no circumstances will any legal responsibility or blame be held against the publisher for any reparation, damages, or monetary loss due to the information herein, either directly or indirectly.

Respective authors own all copyrights not held by the publisher.

The information herein is offered for informational purposes solely, and is universal as so. The presentation of the information is without contract or any type of guarantee assurance.

The trademarks that are used are without any consent, and the publication of the trademark is without permission or backing by the trademark owner. All trademarks and brands within this book are for clarifying purposes only and are the owned by the owners themselves, not affiliated with this document.

INTRODUCTION

I want to appreciate and congratulate you for purchasing the book, "Millionaire Mindset: The Simple Habits And Thinking Behind Money, Wealth, and Success."

This book contains steps and strategies that have been tested and proven on how to acquire and utilize the practices of the very wealthy people in making your own millions.

It also exposes you to the two universal ways by which a millionaire can be identified. Also, you get to find out the big secret behind all that wealth and success.

Lastly, this book will leave you with some food for thought as to why the typical millionaire does not ride the very posh cars or live the very expensive life.

Thanks again for purchasing this book. I hope you enjoy it!

CHAPTER 1
WHO IS A MILLIONAIRE?

"Who wants to be a millionaire?" This is always a catchy phrase, anytime. In fact, for a few folks, they'll rather hit straight for the billions.

But do you really know what it means to be a millionaire? Do you know what qualifies a person to be called a millionaire? We shall find out shortly.

Being a millionaire has to do with the number of assets that you own. Whether these assets are liquid or a function of the net worth of the individual, altogether when valued should sum up to a least a million dollars. The individual is can then be described as a millionaire, and rightly so too.

In other words, a millionaire, when assessed in terms of his net worth, can boast of having at least a million. It could be a million dollars in U.S currency. It could also be a million in another currency that is equal to the dollar.

Notice I have mentioned liquid assets and net worth in my definitions. Let us look at both terms a bit closely.

When the term "net worth" is used, it is always about what a person or an entity owns separate from what it owes. To put differently, it is the entire sum of a person's asset minus the entire sum of his liabilities.

The other part is the liquidity of assets owned. When talking about the liquidity of asset, we are looking at those things an individual owns that are easily convertible to cash. Hold on a bit. Look at it this way.

The stocks that Mr. Smith has is a liquid asset. It is so because he will eventually, whether sooner or later, be converted to cash. He also receives dividends from such investment in the form of cash. It is, therefore, a liquid asset.

If Mr. Smith owns a mansion and a Toyota Camry car, they cannot be viewed as liquid assets. Why? Well, because he actually needs a roof to sleep under. Most likely, he wouldn't like to sell his house to live on the street.

So, a house is an asset all right, but it is not liquid. It is more of a necessity. It doesn't come across to the owner as the first thing to sell off if he needs to settle his children's fees. It is a more long-lasting asset, so to say.

Another example would be his set of clothes. I mean, all things being equal, Mr. Smith would need his clothes for cover and for warmth. He is not likely to sell his clothes in order to feed. If he does so, then what will he wear?

You might want to infer that he does not need to sell all his clothes, maybe just one or two of his designer wears. That, however, is a bit beside the point. The point is his set of clothes are meant to clothe him. It would, therefore, be unlikely for him to simply give up his clothes to buy a bottle of beer, or a plate of salad.

I hope we are getting somewhere with these arguments. Let me cap it up so that we are both on the same page.

We look at a person's stock of liquid assets to declare him a millionaire. That is because those are the near cash assets. We equally look at what a person owns asides what he owes. This tells us what he actually can lay claim to as his property.

Let us view both ways of knowing who a millionaire are two different schools of thoughts. One school supports that a man is a millionaire by virtue of his net worth alone. The other school says that being a millionaire is a function of a man's liquid asset.

Because it is kind of a big deal for me that we are crystal clear about the concept of a millionaire, I would give an example to differentiate both schools of thought.

Imagine that Mr. Smith (that happens to be the name of my favorite high school teacher!) has these stock of assets to his name:

- A house that is worth $600,000
- A car that is worth $12,000
- Funds for retirement worth $500,000
- Stocks which are worth $100,000
- Current market value his furniture and clothes $15,000
- Cash balance $10,000.

This gives his total assets to be $1,237,000

Moving over to his set of liabilities. Imagine that Mr. Smith has some debt in the form of:

- Mortgage loan plus interest worth $130,000
- Outstanding IOU worth $50,000

This makes the total sum of his liabilities to be $180,000.

Now, we start with the first school of thought. Those are the guys who see being a millionaire as having assets less liabilities that is greater than or equal to a million. If we take out the total value of Smith's liabilities from his assets, we would be left with $1,057,000.

The net worth of Mr. Smith, therefore, qualifies him to be called a millionaire. $1,057,000 is over a million dollars. Judging by what the first school of thought upholds then, he is actually a millionaire.

Is it so for the second school?

The second school of thought in our discussion would be the proponents of liquidity of assets as the basis for being a millionaire. If we are to look out only for the liquid aspects of Smith's assets, it would only be his retirement funds, his stocks value, and his cash balances.

Would that sum up to a million dollars? Let's do the math together. $500,000 plus $100,000 plus $10,000 would equal $610,000. This is far less than a million dollars. Oops! Going by the second school, Mr. Smith is nowhere close to being a millionaire (but he is over average at least, I must give to him!)

To reiterate, the market value of his furniture and clothes was exempted from the list of his liquid assets. As I said before, these are less liquid. This means the chances of them being converted to actual cash are quite slim. They are equally indispensable, that is, they are less likely to be done without in the home.

This whole chapter is supposed to set the basis for our further discourse. I didn't mean to bore you with all that math. The aim is simply to settle in your mind (and mine), that we are on the same page as touching who a millionaire is.

From now on we can have a smooth sail. A smooth sail to what mindset a millionaire has. Before we sail, however, I would like to draw your attention to a salient fact.

We have settled on the fact that a millionaire is one who has a total sum of liquid assets worth at least one million dollars. It can also be used for that guy whose net worth is at least one million dollars. But that is not all.

Having one million dollars or one million pounds or one million euros cannot be compared with having one million rupees or naira. This is because of what the last two currencies actually worth in the international market.

It means that a "rich" fellow from Nigerian, that is the one having a million naira may be counted as a middle-income owner in the U.S.

The point I am trying to get at this. The value of individual currencies of nations of the world vary. Some vary greatly when compared to others while some vary not as much. In reference to two of the major currencies of the world, which are the dollar and the pound, all other currencies differ in value.

To be a millionaire in a country is therefore not absolute. A million in one country, owing to the level of inflation prevailing there, may be of far less value. In other words, having a million in some countries would be like living an average life in some other countries.

So, the conventional thing would be to put all millionaires into one major currency; the U.S dollars. This is what should come to mind anytime the word is used all through this book. Millionaires here would refer to those who have at least one million dollars and above as either liquid assets or net worth.

CHAPTER 2
WHAT IS A MILLIONAIRE MINDSET AND HOW IS IT ACQUIRED?

Have you heard that saying? "You have to think rich to be rich." In many instances, this is true. Although, for some rich folks, they were merely born into richness and became rich simply by acquisition.

However, someone had to build that riches for them to acquire. So, in the end, there was a mindset, followed by a series of action which birthed forth the riches.

The Millionaire Mindset

This has to do with the beliefs of very wealthy people that influence what they do and how they act especially as regards their finances. Going from the term "mindset," it is a frame of mind, a way of thinking that is peculiar to the very wealthy class.

This is another way of saying that the wealthy people all think as one. This is especially so when it comes to the way they manage their finances. Let us have a practical look at how the mind of a millionaire actually works.

Point 1: The mind of a millionaire is always focused on his money. This is a must-know fact about millionaires. By being money-focused, the millionaire is not usually given to spending frivolously but amassing consistently.

In other words, the real millionaire is often not out to show off his money. Sometimes you simply know that he is rich by what you have heard of him. Looking at him yourself, you may not be able to arrive at such conclusion.

You can check the statistics. Very many millionaires just drive simple cars and wear simple clothes. This goes especially for those who actually millionaires who are self-made. They have mastered the art of "truly being rich" and not just looking rich.

They are not quick to buy designer boats or posh airplanes. They do not even fancy the very expensive vacation options. I do not mean that they do not want to live the good life, but only a handful of them choose to live the "designer" way.

To put differently, the millionaire focuses on his money. He does not take his mind off it. He is usually not given to spending unproductively. He thinks a whole lot and guess what he thinks about the most? Yes, his money.

The summary of point one is that the real millionaires are very particular about how their money is made and spent. You will find millionaires spending a lot of time thinking about how to grow their wealth. They actually do a lot of thinking in this regard. This is because that is where their focus is.

Point 2: The very wealthy people do not dare to gamble with their money.

The mindset of a millionaire is really about not losing money. In his choices and daily actions, this is very glaring.

The millionaire wants to save up as much as he can from his purchase. He wants to make sure he is buying at the best price. This best price is actually the lowest that he can successfully haggle.

He also is very dogged at selling at the highest price possible. This means that he equally seeks the best price when he sells. Only that in the case of selling, the best price is the highest price he can sell his goods at.

Before I proceed, the last point on not losing money serves as a rule for the millionaire. It is always at the fore of his dealings. There are actually two broad rules that govern a millionaire's mindset. The first is not to lose money.

We have discussed the rule. It doubles as our point two. Now over to rule two.

Rule two says: even when tempted to, be loyal to rule one (were you surprised at this?). I also had to let it settle in myself.

In essence, rule two is to further stress the importance of rule one. We can then say that there is actually one golden rule in the mind of a millionaire. That mindset is to never lose money, period!

Point 3: The millionaire has the mindset of always planning. He plans his finances from the first to the last expense. He is not likely to make any expenditure decision without having first planned for it.

In fact, he is likely to carefully plan for emergencies as well. This is so that serious emergencies, when they arise, have also been planned for. No further planning would be needed to take care of unforeseen contingencies when they finally appear.

We have seen that the millionaire has firstly, the money mindedness. He is glued to his finances. He always seeks to minimize the cost of his expenses and to maximize his business profits. That is why he is an astute planner.

The mind of a millionaire is a mind that plans. While thinking of his account balance, he is planning for every bit of it. Planning is so important to a millionaire that he wants to ensure that even irregular activities are also planned for. Nothing should take him unawares.

Point 4: The mind of the millionaire is a mind that is never in a hurry. One last thing that can be considered a mindset of a millionaire is his firmness on not being in a hurry. Many great millionaires agree that as one investment goes, another comes. They are therefore not pressurized to act hurriedly.

The real millionaires not very interested in making quick decisions, even when it seems the situation warrants such. They prefer to take their time when taking any investment decision. The reason is not far-fetched; they cannot stand to lose their money carelessly.

Point 5: The mindset of a millionaire is set to slowly and steadily acquire more wealth.

The real rich folks are not so much after how quickly they can add up to their wealth. They'd rather increase their wealth slowly and steadily. To them, be slow is preferred to quickly (and with greater risks) trying to amass more wealth. This is one habit that an aspiring millionaire must develop.

We have seen five points that give away the mindset of the millionaire. They define, although not exhaustively, the way a typical millionaire thinks and what informs his practices.

As a follow up from the just concluded discussion, we would examine what habits should be adopted by the millionaire "wannabees."

So, What Habits should the Person Seeking to hit his Millions have?

You may want to ask what the difference between the mindset we have discussed and habits we are about to discuss. The answer is- not much. In fact, you may find some overlapping features as you read on.

But before you pout, just stop to think this through with me. Forming the right habits are a sure way of forming the right mindset. So, while we are out developing the millionaire mindset, we should pick up and stick with the right habits.

Let's begin, shall we?

I once heard a rich fellow once say that the secret to being rich is - there is really no secret. Did that raise your brows a little? When I first heard it, it raised mine.

Let me repeat that statement for emphasis sake. The secret to being rich is that there is no secret. This is the most important phrase I would like you to take out of this entire chapter.

What this key statement means is that if I desire to become a millionaire, I simply do what successful people have done and are doing. Do you see why it is no secret now? At least, they don't hide what they do. After all, they are always in the public view.

With that said, let us highlight a few of the habits that are common to the really wealthy guys.

Getting rich slowly: I just pointed out that fact. The habit of getting rich quickly may not be as effective as that of steadily amassing your thousands. The thousands then sum up to millions. The idea of making one very risky investment so as to hit big is not consistent with the attributes of great millionaires.

Instead of trying to attain those riches quickly, start with managing your finances. Then plan with what you have to achieve that financial freedom. Go over every line of action you intend to take at least thrice. Weigh it through. That would keep you from hurriedly making decisions.

Always seek out good advice: now, this is valuable advice. There are people who currently are where you intend to be. It would be useful to seek their financial advice. You know of great, successful men who started out very small but channeled their resources the right way, why not search them out?

Remember, there is really nothing new. Every strategic plan you intend to use in growing your business must have been considered before, either in the same form or a similar format. Therefore, do not be tempted to act in isolation as regards advice. Seek good advice. It sure cannot hurt you.

Be critical about the investigation: you must be. Investigating every line of investment you intend to tread is as important as making such investment. Again, this will require some time and patience. Your earnings are too precious to go down the drain.

Often, there are investment opportunities that appear very enticing but are truly not the real deal. Proper and due investigation is most likely to uncover which investment is valid and which isn't. I'd like to add here that you should not put yourself under any pressure. Just be calm and composed.

What exactly are you doing to earn money? I chose to save this, for now. However, it is the most crucial point. The fact is that you need something to build upon. Are you currently running a business? Yes, you should. That is where it all begins.

Some funny folks think that they can simply pluck the millions off a money tree or something like that. Well, real millionaires do not think that way. And truly, it doesn't work that way. Get something doing. Do not despise that small business venture. Just stick to doing the little things in the best way.

Moving further

You need that insurance policy: Some people think to themselves, "I have so little, to begin with, do I need to insure anything?" The news is, you actually do. Wealthy people insure against risks.

Due to increase in your business and taking on new ventures or investment opportunities, pick up an insurance policy as well. This is especially needed when that business or investment has some sizeable level of risk.

In truth, paying some amount of money to some insurance guys who may probably not have to repay it can be a tasking thing to do. However, if you look at it from a different, more objective angle, you won't argue that much.

Having a good insurance scheme gives you an aura of confidence. It also keeps you from worrying about unexpected happenings. It could even be that the economy takes a turn for the worse. Still, you have a sure backing of your finances.

Get the services of a lawyer: who says you can do without legal services in your millionaire quest? I didn't – and that's because you sure need a good lawyer. Wealthy folks always have one smart lawyer somewhere helping with the papers. These are one of the things they invest heavily in.

Getting a lawyer as you make your way up the ladder helps to ensure that you do not get into unnecessary lawsuits that can drain all you've got in one scoop. Acting smartly would mean that you have a lawyer who is skilled in estate matters. You also need to consider drawing up a will early too.

One of the benefits of securing good legal services is that they give you expert advice on what form to store your asset. This is so that they do not get seized in the event of a lawsuit.

For example, when the assets of an individual are converted into partnership form, it is not swallowed up nor taxed when something unfavorable happens. It is called covering your assets.

Do not be on the asymmetric end of the information train: what do I mean by that? I simply mean that you should get as much available and necessary information as possible about every expenditure to be made.

It is always best to have detailed information about the full cost of any decision to be made regarding your finances. By full costs, I mean both the explicit and implicit costs of every investment decision.

The explicit costs would imply the prices involved. The implicit cost would refer to the cost of going with that particular investment. Knowing and putting all these costs together would help you make better, well-informed decisions on which financial path to tread.

Be a good negotiator: Millionaires do not always say yes to every price quoted for him simply because he has the means to pay. You shouldn't as well. Always seek to save as much money from every purchase and as much gain on every sale.

We are not saying here that you should exploit people by charging high prices

Definitely not! They will eventually find out, and you may lose your customers.

Being a good negotiator stems from having a good knowledge of general prices, either of the items you purchase or the product you sell. You can then leverage on this information to get the best price at all times for what you buy and sell.

On the purchasing side, you seek lower prices. On the selling side, you seek higher prices. That way you always have something to put away as savings. It also extends to seeking low-interest rates on loans. B sure to do all this with a smile and the right level of confidence.

Do not try to evade taxes: As you aspire to become truly wealthy, do not nurse the idea of evading taxes when you make it big. Come to think of it, being rich does not equate being less responsible. Settle it ahead of time to be a loyal and patriotic citizen, especially with regards to paying tax. The wealthy do!

Do not be afraid to take the initiative: yes, this is a good habit of imbibing. While you must work at not losing money, you must not be afraid to take the bull by the horn. While it is important to avoid losing money at all cost, do not be afraid to make reasonable investments.

Sometimes, you may not hit as much profit as you envisaged. You may even go bankrupt after you have done your research. That should not discourage you from taking initiatives. The truth is that many wealthy people failed woefully at some point in time. They simply kept on keeping on!

In summary, we have seen a few of the habits that you should emulate. They are peculiar to great and successful people. You can adapt and build your mindset around these habits. They will help you in making and keeping those millions.

Why not try them out for yourself today. If you can already boast of having these traits, then keep up with it.

Remember that the secret to success is doing what successful people do. Cheers!

CHAPTER 3

WHY CHOOSE THE MILLIONAIRE MINDSET?

In the previous chapters, we have clearly identified that the secret behind having the wealth and success of millionaires have is simply doing what they do. We also saw a few of the habits of the money making guys. I hope you are willing to try your hands on.

Why should you trail the path of success, wealth and money?

A huge number of millionaires earned their millions by working for it. Only a little fraction of the rich inherited it. What does this show? It shows that the majority of the wealthy people had to work it through, following consistently with their vision to succeed.

You should trail the path to financial freedom because it is achievable. You can become financially free by sticking to the habits and practices of the financially free. You do not need to conjure another means of making your millions, you can simply follow the pattern of beliefs and practices of the already rich folks.

It pays to be financially free: Don't you just love the feeling of being able to plan your future without worrying about the cost implications? The good thing is that you can follow the pattern of those who have gone ahead and are doing very well.

You can actually live out your dreams: knowing that there is a mindset that millionaires live by is another way of saying that that can live that way and become a millionaire. This is just to say that a millionaire is a normal person who has stuck with the principles of financial success. If you can stick with it, you can make it right to the very top.

To end this chapter, I would like to leave you with some food for thought. I was at a fix as touching where to place this category of attributes or do I say advice. I decided to make it as a stand-alone. Let me title it;

Some piece of advice

Diligence, patience, and a clear vision is a necessity: It is important to know that seeking to become a millionaire overnight is not ideal. If that is the case, then you will have to patiently work your way to the freedom you desire financially.

Exercising patience is important. This would keep you from making hasty decisions. You need diligence. This will help you be detailed and informed about every financial decision you make. Lastly, a clear vision of your goal is required.

A clear vision keeps you from being distracted. It also gives you the drive to continue with your goal even when you face stunt challenges. A clear vision will make you unstoppable and dauntless until your goal of being a millionaire is achieved.

Keep your focus: With your vision clear, you need to keep your focus. Vision and focus are not the same things. However, they are complementary. Be clear about what you want- that is your vision. Then, be focused on your vision.

Your focus will keep you asking questions and evaluating your decisions regularly. Successful people will tell you they never lost their focus. You shouldn't as well. Staying focused keeps you thinking. It would keep your thought pattern productive.

Have a mentor: Yes, you need one. You need to sit under the person whose success level you admire and desire to acquire. We have repeatedly said that there is no new secret to success. It is the same thing that is done by the same people who are successful.

So, the secret you need is to simply copy and replicate what successful people have done. To make it more effective, choose a particular person who is truly successful.

You can try to contact them. If you can't, try to get hold of their books. You could also read up their biography, attend seminars where they are featured and even watch their videos if available. All of this is to keep you tuned and connected to what made that person thick. And then, be sure to copy it!

Appreciate every progress that you make in view of your goal: It is good to keep this in mind; no success is a small success! Every milestone crossed on your way to that big dream should not be jettisoned. Every success, however little, is worth celebrating. Celebrate the progress you have made, it will prop you up to run with your vision.

Many wealthy people point to the secret of their wealth as being the millionaire mindset. You can also follow through with this mindset, doing the right things and keep the right habits.

See you at the very top!

CONCLUSION

Thank you once again for purchasing this book!

I hope this book was able to help you grasp the two different ways by which a millionaire can be known. I also hope you were able to pick out the habits and practices of the wealthy class.

You must have also spotted that the secret to success and wealth is doing what the wealthy and successful do. Get the go for it today!

Finally, if you enjoyed this book, then I'd like to ask you for a favor, would you be kind enough to leave a review for this book? It'd be greatly appreciated.

Thank you and good luck.

Printed in Great Britain
by Amazon